Make the Connection

5 Ways Smart Leaders Build Strong Organizations

LIZ URAM

ISBN-13: 978-1981884810
ISBN-10: 1981884815

DEDICATION

To the organizations and individuals who have shared their
experiences with me and to those who have allowed me
the privilege of sharing my experiences with them.

CONTENTS

ACKNOWLEDGMENTS

As always, my appreciation goes out to my husband Todd for his never-ending support and belief in me and my work. To our children Chelsea, Jessica, Denzel, and Devon who inspire me to be a good role model as they make their mark on the world.

INTRODUCTION

The executive team just returned from a quarterly offsite planning session with a popular one page strategic plan in hand. After two days with a highly paid consultant, the plan was neatly and succinctly organized. The team was pleased with themselves, as they should have been for doing the work, but when it came time to roll the plan out to the rest of the organization they hesitated. They knew the next step was to pass the plan on to the next level of management for implementation but they weren't sure how and they knew it would require more than a brief hand off. When it came time to advance the plan to the next stage, they discovered that the once well-defined organizational goals were hazy and no one could quite recall which team was going to take ownership. The plan that seemed so clear at the retreat now looked a little vague. They had a strategic plan in place with no idea how to translate it into tactical plans of action.

This scenario plays out in offices of both for profit and non-profit organizations of all sizes in all industries during the annual or quarterly planning period. After a strenuous session of strategic planning, the team produces a document that is complex yet vague, and it never makes it beyond the top tier of the organization. The most critical aspect of putting a strategic plan in place is the implementation of that plan.

There is no shortage of good methods to guide the top leaders of an organization on how to create the overall strategic plan. Unfortunately, those great methods can lose traction when it comes to implementation. Without implementation all you have is a plan, not results.

Make the Connection picks up where most strategic planning methods leave off and provides a method for translating organizational strategy into tactical plans for implementation.

If the top leaders in the company need help to put the plan in place, how is everyone else supposed to inherently know what to do? Make the Connection focuses on how to filter the completed plan through the organization for implementation and makes sure all pieces fit together.

Make the Connection is the definitive book for performance-based organizations that are serious about achieving results through executing on strategy. Performance-based organizations know the true meaning of the saying 'work smarter, not harder' and they focus on results, clarity, and action all of which result in efficient and productive operations.

I've had the privilege of working with thousands of

employees representing hundreds of organizations and one theme that has come through loud and clear is that people want to feel connected. This is true in organizations of all sizes and all types. From manufacturing to non-profits, government agencies to corporate offices, and everything in between, people want to know what's going on.

Connection comes through communication. So many organizations are struggling with employee engagement issues because of a lack of communication.

Simplicity is the ultimate form of sophistication

– *Leonardo da Vinci*

This book encourages simplicity. Simplicity worries some people. They are so used to everything being complex that when a simple idea is presented they assume something must be missing or that the idea couldn't possibly work because it is just too simple.

It concerns me when I hear about organizations that implement methods to increase efficiencies only to find that people are working longer hours than they were before the so-called efficiencies were implemented. The words efficiency and longer hours do not belong in the same sentence. It's an oxymoron and doesn't make sense yet it happens all the time.

One department at one of the largest financial corporations in the U.S. requires its employees to print off their emails at the end of each day in case catastrophe strikes the office during the night. That is the ultimate in wastefulness of time and money. Apparently they don't realize they have backup servers in case of such an emergency.

Efficiencies are meant to improve the workload and therefore a reduction in hours worked would seem obvious. On the other hand, no matter how much you strive to improve efficiencies some people just won't have it. Some people wear the burden of extended work hours like a badge of honor. I don't think that will be the case for anyone to whom this book appeals. If you are consistently working more hours than you'd like, take heart, if you apply the information applied in this book you will find you can be more productive in less time than you are now and you will achieve better results.

Too often, simple methods and ideas for improvements end up as complex beasts that do the exact opposite of what was intended. After reading and applying the ideas in this book you'll see that simple is the smart the way to go. There is nothing wrong with achieving results through simple methods. After all, what would you rather have an overcomplicated plan that doesn't get implemented or a simple completed plan? The answer is obvious.

Political campaigns and debates are a perfect example of too much talk and not enough action. Candidates who come out with simple plans are mocked for being naïve but if you listen to the politicians with the lengthy discourses they aren't actually saying anything at all. They are all talk and no walk as my mother always says.

Through my work I've discovered three main reasons for the disconnect between strategy and implementation. These reasons are so common that it would be rare if your organization wasn't experiencing at least one of them. With a little effort you can easily bridge the gap and execute on the plan.

Reason #1 – Lack of Alignment

Make the Connection is a simple approach intended to ensure that individual efforts are aligned with the company goals. An organization can have the best strategic plan in the world but if the individuals who are actually doing the work have no clue what the plan is the chances of achieving the desired results are slim.

Reason #2 – Lack of Direction

Make the Connection creates the right conditions for a fully engaged work force from top to bottom. An engaged workforce is one where everyone understands their role and responsibilities and how the work they do adds to the success of the organization. Gallup research reveals that 70% of the American workforce is disengaged.

Reason #3 – Lack of Ownership

Make the Connection promotes a culture of accountability through personal responsibility. It is not doing for employees what they can do for themselves, it is empowering employees to do for themselves with the proper guidance.

Make the Connection is the first step to connecting the pieces of what the organization wants – productivity and profitability – and what the employee wants – communication and purpose. Organizations achieve results when there is a clear connection between strategy and execution.

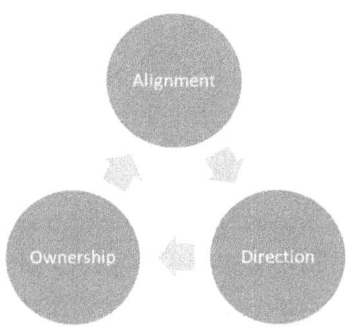

Roles and responsibilities of the connected team

One of the goals of this book is to examine and define the responsibilities of each level in the organization. Every role is vital to the success of the company. An important and often missing link in bridging the gap between strategy and execution is transparency about the roles and responsibilities of each person.

When I started writing this book the plan was to write one big leadership volume that covered top level leadership to mid-level managers to individual contributors. As the words formed on the pages I decided to split the book into three shorter volumes to make it easier to digest.

Starting at the top, this book, *Make the Connection*, details five ways top-level leaders can build a strong team that is connected from top to bottom. You will discover how to clarify and communicate your primary purpose, get the team to buy-in to the *why* behind the *what*, simply define a core belief system, understand the real personality of your organization, and put the overall plan into action.

The next book, *Communicate Like a Boss*, covers five ways smart managers connect with their team through clear communication. This book covers setting expectations, goal setting, delegation, coaching, and motivation. In my own experience and that of others, these are the skills that are most challenging for managers and the ones that have the biggest return when they master them.

Finally, *The Power of Personal Leadership* focuses on five principles everyone can develop to become a better leader, regardless of title. Topics covered include: self-awareness, positive attitude, time management, resiliency, and dealing with difficult people. I chose these topics because in my own experience and in working with others, these are the areas that cause the most problems in the workplace.

Everyone in the organization has a role and everyone's role must be clearly defined for optimal performance. Titles may vary depending on the organizational structure of your company but the idea remains the same. Senior leaders set the strategy, managers give direction that leads to implementation, individual contributors do the work.

Frustration rises when priorities shift or changes are put in place that people don't understand. What individual contributors, and even some managers, sometimes fail to realize is that it's the job of the leader to look at the organization from the highest level and look down the road to what's ahead and that can require a change in direction. Sometimes very quickly. While the individual contributor is focused on what's happening right here and now the executive level is looking into the future.

One way to create a connection is to describe the roles and responsibilities of each level and help each person see how their role fits in to the bigger picture.

The following illustration shows the roles and responsibilities in a typical hierarchial organizational structure. Your organization may not look exactly like this in terms of number of levels or titles but the responsibilites are fundamental to any structure.

Role

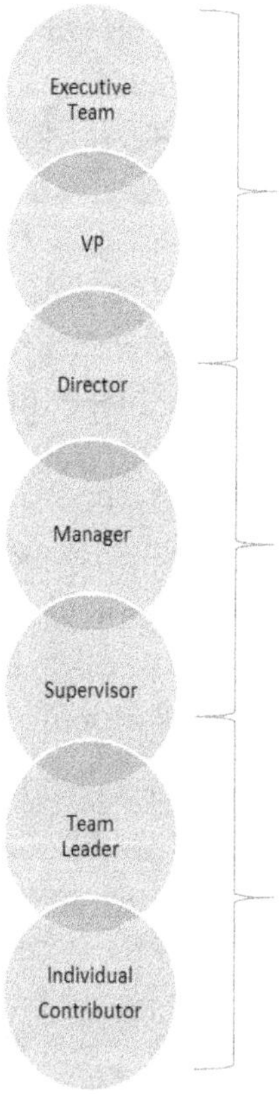
Executive Team
VP
Director
Manager
Supervisor
Team Leader
Individual Contributor

Responsibility

Alignment
- Vision
- Mission
- Values
- Culture
- Strategy

Direction
- Goals
- Standards
- Coaching
- Delegation
- Motivation

Execution
- Self-awareness
- Attitude
- Resilience
- Time Management
- Conflict Management

With so many different roles and responsibilities, it's no wonder it's so easy to get disconnected in the workplace. Role confusion is one of the top causes of break downs in communication. Everyone in the organization should read all sections of the book to help shed light on the differences in the types of work performed at each level.

As St. Francis of Assisi prayed, centuries before Stephen Covey spread the philosophy by putting it into print in the classic 7 Habits of Highly Effective People, 'Help me not so much to be understood, as to understand". This book will help you do just that.

A team is a group of individuals working toward the same goal. Ideally, each individual brings a unique set of gifts and abilities to the team and each person is valued for how their contributions help to make the team great. Sadly, instead of valuing each person, there is a strange idea that everyone has to be the same and a great deal of effort goes into leveling the playing field to make everyone the same. I dislike the old saying there is no I in team because without the individual me's there would be no team. Each individual must do their part to contribute to the overall success.

Team's go bad when people get caught up in what other people are doing and lose focus on doing their part.

Case in point: I was brought in to a company to conduct a team building session for a team that was experiencing severe conflict. No one was taking personal responsibility and each individual was more focused on what other members of the team were doing or not doing than what they were doing.

Everyone claimed that they were the only ones doing the work. They were in extreme finger pointing mode. A team building workshop could not help them. They didn't need team building, they needed to learn ownership and personal responsbility. Once the fundamentals of individual ownership are in place, then you can build a strong team but not before.

Successful teams are developed out of a shared desire to reach a common goal. Each individual understands their role in achieiving the results and accepts what they need to do to make it happen.

How to use this book

This book is meant to be practical and informative. You will find specific instructions on how to apply the information from each chapter and how to make the connection when making the handoff to the next level. The ideas set forth in this book work for organizations of all types and sizes. Large organizations simply cascade the model throughout each division or department of the organization. While a large organization may have multiple levels of the model, a small organization may have just one.

CHAPTER 1

CONNECTION STARTS AT THE TOP

Everything rises and falls on leadership

– *John Maxwell*

When the third-generation owner of a truck dealership passed away unexpectedly in 2010, his widow had a big decision to make and only 180 days to make it. She had been a stay-at-home mom for the previous 15 years and now had to decide whether to take over a business which, until that point, her involvement was limited to serving on the board of directors or sell it. Not an easy decision to make while still reeling from the unexpected loss of her husband and adjusting to her new way of life. Nor was it a simple matter of signing off on paperwork to reassign ownership.

Changing ownership of the dealership through the parent company would require submitting herself through a strenuous approval process. Not

14

one to shy away from a challenge, her determination came through and she decided to go through the steps needed to convince the parent company that she was a qualified successor. She succeeded in her bid and is now the president and CEO of one of the largest truck dealerships in the nation.

When she took over, she did something that some leaders never do in their entire career, and was not done at her own company until then. She put together a strategic plan for moving the business forward.

For more than 80 years the business succeeded under a traditional command and control style of management. Many people would look at that history and stick with the tried and true. I asked her why she did it. Why she was willing to put the work into improving something that was already working. She said she did it to sustain their competitive advantage.

She saw a need for a different style of leadership to take them into the future. While she knew her own strengths, she also knew her limitations so she sought professional advice from a local university where they recommended the implementation of certain structures that would be necessary to sustain future growth.

She knew their competitive advantage would come from increasing sales, attracting quality management, and maintaining a well-run company and those things required structure and strategy. A 250% increase in truck sales since the former stay-at-home mom came on board is proof that strategy makes a difference.

The number one responsibility of a leader is to drive the overall alignment of the organization. What the leader does and says is what everyone else will do and say. In the game follow the leader, one kid is picked to be the leader and the rest of the kids form a line and follow the leader wherever they go. If the leader goes right, everyone goes right. If the leader goes left, everyone goes left. If the leader just stands there and does nothing, everyone else will stand there and do nothing and the game is over. If the leader passes off their responsibility they lose their position and become a follower. The leader is always at the front of the line paving the way.

In the 360 Leader, John Maxwell says,

"The strength of any organization is a direct result of the strength of its leaders. Weak leaders equal weak organizations. Strong leaders equal strong organizations. Everything rises and falls on leadership."

If you want to know why a company is doing

well or not so well all you have to do is look to the top. This is known as top down leadership. The leaders, whether they realize it or not, set the tone for the rest of the company.

A leader who ignores issues, who is absent, or who doesn't have a vision, creates an atmosphere of distrust and confusion.

A leader who claims ignorance is no leader at all. A leader must take full responsibility for every action taken under his or her management. Responding to issues with 'I didn't know' is a weak excuse for a leader. Conversely, a leader who has a clear vision, sets clear expectations, and holds people accountable will create conditions that allow for people to be extraordinary.

At the head of any organization you will find the top tier management. This includes, but is not limited to, the chief executive officer or president, and the executive team including chief operating officer, chief information officer, chief financial officer, chief marketing officer, and chief compliance officer, to name a few.

If the organization is a non-profit the top level might be the executive director. You may also find multiple variations of vice presidents (vp, svp, evp, etc.) in this tier, along with directors. The assortment of titles are many and they vary depending on the size and type of the organization.

Certain professions such as attorneys, accountants, and wealth managers, usually have the title of partner. Whatever the title, the role of the top tier is to create alignment by identifying the destination of the organization.

Titles don't matter as much as span of responsibility, I only mention them as a means to help identify who is in the top tier of the organization. I learned a long time ago not to put too much weight into titles.

I received this lessson the day the head of the division I worked in stopped by to let me know my assistant vice president (AVP) designation had been approved. He said 'you know it doesn't mean anything don't you'. Not what I wanted to hear at the time but wise words and a lesson that has always stuck with me. He didn't say it to put me down, he said it to give me perspective. And probably to keep my ego in check.

As you read, keep in mind that because the connected model scales, this section applies to anyone who is leading other people. If you are a department manager or even someone who aspires to lead someday, and I hope that many of you are, you can apply this information regardless of your title or level of responsibility.

Let's be clear about one thing up front... businesses exist for one reason: to make a profit. Achieving profitability is the main responsibility of the top tier of leadership. Even non-profits have to be concerned about the bottom line or they won't be able to provide their services.

Without profitability the organization can't exist, and if the organization doesn't exist neither do the jobs and products or services it provides.

It's no wonder so many leadership books use metaphors for exploration such as navigating, true north, ocean, and unchartered territory. When it comes to achieving profitability there is no certainty. Talk about the wild blue yonder. Profitability depends on many uncertain factors including market conditions, consumer spending, technology, and competition to name a few.

Leadership roles are typically occupied by people of vision. This is natural since it takes vision to anticipate what's coming up and stay ahead of the curve. This can cause frustration in the organization because visionaries tend to verbalize their ideas causing others to assume that they should stop what they are working on, change course, and start working on the latest and greatest idea that the leader mentioned. That isn't necessarily the case.

In *Rocket Fuel*, the authors refer to this as whiplash. Whiplash occurs when an organization is so tuned in to what the leader is thinking that it causes unintended changes in direction. One minute everyone is focused on *this* shiny object and the next minute they're focused on *that* shiny object.

Shifting of priorities is a common source of frustration in the workplace and can be extremely demotivating to an employee who has been working hard on completing a project only to have it put on hold or cancelled all together only to begin work on something new. This kind of behavior can leave the employee feeling like the rug has been pulled out from under him. When this behavior continues over a long period of time and becomes the norm, it can lead to reduced morale which leads to decreased productivity. People may begin to acquire an apathetic attitude and think 'Why bother putting all my effort in to this project since it will probably get put on hold anyway?'. Once this attitude becomes part of the culture it can be very difficult to turn around.

Make no mistake, a culture like this was created from the top down. The employee gets resentful at the constant change and the manager wonders how the great employee turned out to be such a dud, and conflict grows.

It's doubtful that the visionary leader intended this to happen when they offhandedly shared their latest, greatest idea at the last all-staff team meeting or in a passing hallway conversation.

The authors of *Rocket Fuel* go on to advise that to avoid this disruptive phenomenon, both leaders and followers need to be aware of this tendency and come up with a plan for knowing when to act and when to ignore the ideas the visionary is casually tossing out. The leaders should be open to answering clarifying questions and the people affected should make the effort to ask the clarifying questions rather than make assumptions.

The following is an example of what can go wrong when clarifying questions are not asked:

A large financial institution was redesigning its employee intranet. The head of the company happened to mention that he wanted the key performance indicators (KPIs) to be accessible from the front page. Instead of asking a few clarifying questions, someone interpreted this to mean that the focus of the *entire* front page should be the KPIs. All the work that had been done up until that point, which was significant, was scrapped to make the change. When the new design was rolled out, the leader was surprised to see the KPIs prominently featured on the front page because all he really wanted was a link on the front page for easy access.

Imagine how much time and money this cost the company. Not to mention the discouragement on the part of the team who had been working hard on this project only to have their efforts stripped away. This is a prime example of a disconnect and one that is all too common in organizations.

To sum up the role of the leader, the leader is responsible for where the organization is going and the overall health of the organization. Unless the organization is very small and the leader is playing dual roles of visionary and executor, the leader is not charged with figuring out how they will get there. A good leader surrounds him or herself with people who know how to get things done.

Strategy without tactics is the slowest route to victory. Tactics without strategy is the noise before defeat.

– Sun Tzu, The Art of War

Strategy for the overall organization is the long-term vision set at the executive level. It's the big idea. But too often the strategy doesn't get filtered down through the rest of the company so the disconnect starts at the very top. The employees who have to do the work need to know what the plan is in order to execute on it. If they don't, the chances that the individual work will align with the company strategy is slim.

Keep in mind that when I refer to employees throughout this book, I am talking about all employees at all levels. Anyone who is collecting a paycheck is considered an employee. You may be an owner, executive or manager reading this book but if you are collecting a paycheck you are also an employee.

Strategy is one of those slippery words that can be difficult to define. Strategy starts as a long-term vision that at some point becomes tactical. It has to or nothing happens.

Here's a helpful explanation from dictionary.com that differentiates between strategy and tactics:

> In military usage, a distinction is made between <u>strategy</u> and <u>tactics</u>. Strategy is the utilization, during both peace and war, of all of a nation's forces, through large-scale, long-range planning and development, to ensure security or

victory. Tactics deals with the use and deployment of troops in actual combat.

Another way to say it is that strategy is the overall plan while tactics are the day to day activities. Being strategic and being tactical are not mutually exclusive. You can be both but not at the same time.

Strategy and tactics are two very different things. It's like comparing apples to oranges. I can walk and I can ride a bike but I can't walk and ride a bike at the same time.

You won't get very far in life if you can't put action steps to your big idea. As an individual you probably use strategy and tactics all the time in your personal life without putting much thought into it.

Take celebrating a special occasion as an example. You start with an idea of what you want the celebration to look like and what you hope to accomplish [strategy]. You picture the evening, the mood, and the look on the guest of honor's face. If you stop with that image it's just a good idea. The big idea has to morph into action to come to fruition so you take the proper steps make it happen [tactics]. You set the date and choose the venue, plan the menu, and invite the guests, and so on until the anticipated occasion arrives and you sit down to enjoy the fruits of your labor. What started as an idea [strategy] became an achievement because you acted [tactics] on the idea. That's the flow from strategy to implementation.

It's one thing to make a clean pass from the big idea to the individual action when you are doing it all yourself but it gets a little more complicated when you bring other people into the mix. (Note: you can find specific steps on how to delegate in 'Communicate Like a Boss', available on Amazon.)

The transition from strategy to tactics is bar none the biggest risk for disconnect in an organization. This is when the communication falls apart and the plan that seemed so clear has become a little hazy.

Tactics require a different type of thinking than strategy. It's the difference between a bird's eye view from 30,000 feet – the leaders range of vision; and seeing three feet in front of you – the individual contributor's responsibility.

Strategy can be viewed as *what* we're doing and tactics can be viewed as *how* we're doing it.

At the intersection of strategy and tactics are the one year goals. If you could only choose one stage of the strategy to communicate to the rest of the company, choose the one year goals.

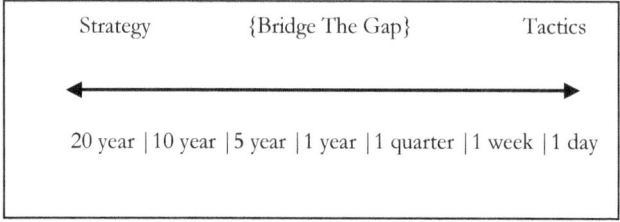

Strategy	{Bridge The Gap}	Tactics

20 year | 10 year | 5 year | 1 year | 1 quarter | 1 week | 1 day

The one year goals are the mark that all employees should stake their individual goals on.

Whose job is it to set strategy and whose job is it to put the strategy in motion? The executive team, advisory board, and board of directors, or any mix thereof put the strategy in place.

The direction for implementing the specific tactics are given by the senior leaders, managers, supervisors, and the individual contributors put the tactics in action.

Make The Connection

At the end of each chapter you'll find information on how to make the connection by communicating and cascading to the next level. There are a variety of ways to do this and you'll find good, better, and best practices for doing so.

The information in this book scales to fit all sizes of organizations and can be applied to smaller segments within the organization itself. If you are a manager of a department you can easily apply these ideas to your area regardless of what is happening in other areas. In fact, applying these ideas at the department level would be very good practice because you can develop your skills without a great amount of risk.

The ideal situation is one where the ideas are applied to the organization as a whole and are then cascaded down within each division and department. The detail and scope may decrease as you go down each level but the general principles are the same.

The purpose is to create a clear road map that spells out the destination, purpose, values, and goals for your area of responsibility. It creates something concrete that people can get their arms around. As mentioned above, learning these practices early on helps develop the skills of the up and coming leaders.

Any fool can make things more complex. It takes a touch of genius to move in the opposite direction.

– Albert Einstein

Resist the urge to overcomplicate the

process. People don't intentionally overcomplicate things, they just can't believe that a simple idea can work so they add to it until it's full of fluff.

The process doesn't need to be perfect but it does require application and follow through. Take a step and move on. Better to have a couple of clearly written ideas that can be incorporated and discussed than to spend weeks or months agonizing over a perfectly written mission statement that no on can understand or remember.

5 Ways Smart Leaders Build Strong Organizations

The 5 responsbilities of the leader are to define:

1. Vision – our primary purpose
2. Mission – why we do it
3. Values – what we believe
4. Culture – who we are
5. Goals – how we will get there

Key points:

- Every organization rises or falls on leadership
- Leadership requires vision
- Leaders drive alignment
- At the intersection of strategy and execution are the one year goals

Notes

Notes

_____

_____

_____

_____

_____

_____

_____

_____

_____

_____

_____

_____

_____

_____

_____

_____

_____

_____

_____

_____

_____

_____

_____

_____

_____

_____

_____

CHAPTER 2

DEFINE THE PRIMARY PURPOSE

Good business leaders create a vision, articulate the vision, passionately own the vision, and relentlessly drive it to completion.

– Jack Welch

In 2001, Paul Johnson found himself face to face with the old saying 'when one door closes, another one opens'.

When Paul was let go from his position as general manager of a large manufacturing facility, job security was top of mind. The layoff happened right after 9/11 and there was a lot of uncertainty in the market. As he weighed his options, he decided he didn't want to settle for another job working for someone else with an uncertain future so he crafted a vision of starting a national company with a sound reputation and a mission to create an environment where job security was a top priority.

As the idea became more of a reality he knew he couldn't pull it off alone so he put together a team of five guys with complementary skills and shared the vision with them. In 2002, the six partners officially launched Aggressive Hydraulics and since then they have seen their vision become a reality. They are a growing national company with 66 employees and big plans for the future.

The first component of alignment is defining and communicating the primary purpose, or vision. A leaders job is to lead, and to do that a leader must have a destination in mind. Because the entire well-being of the organization starts at the top, it is essential that the leader take ownership of the overall vision for the organization and communicating the vision to everyone else. The vision is typically shared by means of a written vision statement.

Unfortunately, vision statements have become nothing more than a check box on the strategic plan for many organizations. They have become hyped up, overcomplicated, and frothy. Something to complete for the sake of completion, framed, and hung in the lobby. For these reasons alone, many people detest them and dread the idea of having to sit through the process of defining the vision.

Sometimes a consultant is brought in to facilitate the process and it makes it worse. There's an old joke that the more convoluted and meaningless the vision statement, the more money it cost to produce. It goes back to what I mentioned earlier – simpler is better.

When we bring it back to basics we find that vision statements do have an actual and beneficial purpose. A vision statement answers the question of 'What is our primary purpose?'. It gives people something to hang their hat on, a foundation to build off. Having a foundation creates energy and excitement.

Sharing the vision helps ensure the whole team is on the same page. If the entire team is not clear on the primary purpose of the organization or department they won't get very far.

This was painfully illustrated in a professional football game at the end of the 2015 season. The game went into overtime which required a fresh coin toss to determine which team would possess the ball first.

The captain of the team making the call got confused and deferred the ball to the other team.

The opposing team scored on their first drive ending the game and the team's hopes.

After the game a reporter asked the head coach what happened and he responded that he had no idea why the captain made that call. They were not on the same page and it cost them not only the game but a spot in the playoffs as well.

Authors of *The Orange Revolution,* Adrian Gostick and Chester Elton, explain the importance of sharing the vision as follows:

> ... in the absence of a defined overarching reason for being, members come up with their own agendas. The resulting mishmash of competing personal goals places teammates at cross purposes, triggers rivalries and turf wars, and can even prompt co-worker sabotage. In the most extreme cases, people desert their teams, either by leaving physically or by checking out mentally and emotionally.

Minimizing the risk of rivalries, wars, and sabotage sounds like a compelling reason to share the vision. It's likely that we've all found ourselves in a position of competing priorities at some point in our lives because each person wanted his or her own way rather than sharing a common goal.

Have you ever shared paddling duties in a canoe with someone else only to find the craft veering off to one side or actually going in circles? Even the most casual trip down the river requires a good deal of coordination and shared vision to keep the little craft in line. If one rower wants to go over to the left bank of the river and the other person wants to rest on the island in the middle you will find yourself in a tug of war that can't be won. When the rowers aren't in sync you can't make much progress. That's how it is for any team.

Before every shot, I go to the movies.

– Jack Nicklaus, Professional Golfer

Professional and olympic athletes often attribute the use of visualization techniques to their success. They carefully hold a detailed picture in their mind of what they are going to do and can see it happening before it actually comes to pass. In other words, they play the movie in their minds.

Vision is by nature, and definition, visual. Therefore, it can be difficult to put it in to words. That is one of the reasons you see so many poorly written vision statements.

As is often the case with other aspects of strategy, the vision statement can be overcomplicated and at the same time vague. We think it needs to be more complex than it does. If we manage to get a simple idea down on paper we look at it and think 'that can't possibly be enough'. It is. Simplicity is best. Go easy on fluffy adjectives and heavy on concrete ideas.

Vision is the art of seeing what is invisible to others.

– Jonathan Swift

Articulating the vision can be difficult. It requires being able *say* what you *see* so others can see it too.

Did you ever cloud-gaze as a kid? Do you remember what is was like to lie in the thick green grass under a bright blue sky dotted with puffy clouds on a perfect summer day with a gentle breeze blowing by? You could lie there for hours and use your imagination to visualize different objects. Did you ever to describe the formation you saw to your friend only to find out that they saw the same cloud very differently than you did? Where you saw a fierce dragon they saw a cat. That's what it can be like when you try to articulate your vision to others.

Defining the vision takes imagination, faith, and good communication skills. You have to put an idea into place that doesn't currently exist. Because you are pulling the idea out of thin air, you need a great deal of faith to believe it will happen. And lastly, you have to find a way to persuade others to get on board with your idea and that requires the ability to turn abstract ideas into concreate ideas. The following exercise will show you how to create a clear, concise statement.

Writing The Vision Statement

There are three components to include in the vision statement:

1. verb

2. noun

3. where

Use active verbs such as achieve, make, do, be instead of passive verbs like maintain or retain.

Identify what you are working toward with a

noun. The noun could be a thing, an achievement, a position.

The where indicates the location. It could be worldwide, national, local, or something specific like an Olympic podium. Here are some examples:

Example	Verb	Noun	Where
Microsoft	Put	Computer	Every desk and home
GE	Be	#1 or #2	Field
Olympian	Win	Gold Medal	Olympics
Sales Team	Achieve	Sales Goals	Company
Zappos	Create	Website	Shoes

Use the following guide to generate ideas for your vision. Write down as many different words as you can think of in each column.

Don't worry about crafting the perfect sentence as this point. Just brainstorm as many different words as you can. After you've exhausted your vocabulary, select the best ones from each column and make a sentence out of it.

The creative process is messy but when the vision statement is articulated it will be clear where you are going.

Verb	Noun	Where
Be	*#1 cable provider*	*In the country*

Microsoft's vision from it's early days is an example of a well-articulated vision. It was a succinct statement about what they were trying to accomplish:

Put a computer on every desk and in every home.

It just doesn't get any simpler, or clear, than that. According to the U.S. Census bureau, (https://www.census.gov/history/pdf/acs-internet2013.pdf) in 2013, 83.8 percent of U.S. households reported computer ownership. Sounds like Microsoft is making progress.

Here's another example from another great American company:

According to *Welch, An American Icon,* (Lowe, J. (2001). New York: John Wiley & Sons, Inc.)

throughout his tenure as CEO of General Electric, Jack Welch urged his division leaders to be the best. If the company which they led was not number one or two in their field then it would be sold. That directive spurred his company presidents to action. The vision for each division of GE was, you could say, to be number one or number two in their field.

Who should write the vision? The leadership team. There are times when group buy-in is appropriate and times when the leadership team needs to take charge. Crafting the vision is one of the times when the top level leadership needs to take charge.

Best practices for writing the vision

- Keep it to one sentence. The examples from Microsoft and GE above are one sentence each. If they can do it, so can you.
- Avoid words that explain how the vision will be achieved. Vision is what you will do, not how you will do it.
- Exclude timeframes. Vision is long-term and may never have a definite end. Although the vision has some characteristics of a goal, it intentionally lacks timeframes. It's something you

are working toward. You will put timeframes around the goals that you'll put in place to move toward the vision. Think of the vision as the ideal to work toward.

Make the Connection – Communicate and Cascade

In the best-selling strategic planning book *Traction*, author Gino Wickman says 'the number one reason employees don't share a company vision is that they don't know what it is'. If you don't tell them, who will? Don't blame the employees for not searching out the framed fluff in the lobby or on the company website. Give it to them in simple terms everyone can get their heads around.

Make the connection by communicating and cascading the vision throughout the organization from top to bottom.

Starting at the top, share the vision during company-wide employee meetings and in meetings with direct reports. Say something like, 'Our primary purpose at ABC Digital Technology is to be the #1 provider of cutting-edge technology in the United States".

Use the vision as a baseline for showing progress or supporting change initiatives. When reviewing a proposal for a change initiative submitted from someone else, request that it clearly prove how the change supports the vision.

Keep the vision front and center to ensure

alignment.

Cascade the vision by having the next level create a vision for their area. As the vision cascades down it might become narrower in scope.

Mid-level managers can take the same steps as outlined above to communicate and cascade the vision to their departments.

Keep the vision in the forefront of discussions during staff meetings and when communicating change. When announcing change, make the connection to show how the change supports the overall vision.

Look for ways to connect the vision to the work the team is doing.

Cascade the vision by creating a vision for your own area of responsibility. If the overall vision is to be number one in the industry, the vision for the sales team might be to exceed their sales goals every year. That department vision has a direct connection to the overall vision of becoming number one in the industry.

What if you are a director or manager at a company that does not have a crisp, clear vision in place coming down from the top? View it for what it is, an opportunity to create clarity for your team.

There is no harm in defining a vision for your

own team. Leaders at every level should take on this responsibility for their own area regardless if it is being done at the level above. Ideally, there is a clearly articulated vision for the organization as a whole but even if there is a poorly articulated vision or no vision at all, you can still create one for your area.

Good, Better, or Best?

It's been said that the good is the enemy of the best. That means it can be easy to settle for good enough rather than taking the time and energy into being the best.

A good question to ask ourselves frequently is 'How much better could we be?'.

GOOD

Verbally share the vision at the company-wide employee meeting and publish the overall organizational vision on the company website, in marketing material, corporate reports, and in the lobby.

BETTER

Communicate to the company as a whole, *and* develop and display department specific vision statements in each department.

BEST

Communicate to the company as a whole, develop department specific statements, *and* display the cascading vision for each area of the organization from top to bottom for internal use.

Consider a visual display to feature the vision for each level of the organization. Ideally, where you hold all staff meetings for easy reference. It could look something like this....

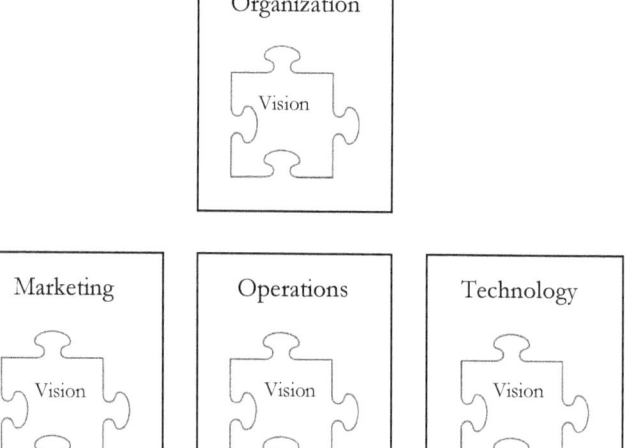

The above diagram is for illustration only. Add as many pieces as needed to represent your organization. Add additional pieces under each level to show the connection by department or team. Individuals don't have to create their own vision.

A puzzle piece as a visual is optional, use whatever design makes sense for your organization. The purpose is to encourage ownership by making the connection throughout all levels of the organization.

Key Concepts

- The vision statement answers the question 'What is our primary purpose?'
- A shared vision provides a sense of direction.
- Write the vision statement in one sentence and include a verb, noun, and place.
- Cascade the vision and share it internally.

Don't wait to be great. Create a vision for your area and yourself regardless of whether it has been done at the level above you.

Notes

Notes

_____

_____

_____

_____

_____

_____

_____

_____

_____

_____

_____

_____

_____

_____

_____

_____

_____

_____

_____

_____

_____

_____

_____

_____

_____

_____

_____

_____

CHAPTER 3

THE WHY BEHIND THE PURPOSE

When you discover your mission, you will its demand. It will fill you with enthusiasm and a burning desire to get to work on it.

– W. Clement Stone

If vision answers the question 'What is our primary purpose?', then mission answers the question 'Why?'. The connected team knows *why* they are doing *what* they are doing.

One of the most important reasons for defining the mission is that it provides focus. The mission helps ensure that all actions align with the primary purpose.

In the day to day busyness of the workplace it's easy to lose focus of *why* we are doing *what* we are doing. The mission can be a simple reminder of the work required to get the job done.

Today's workplace is full of changing priorities and it's easy to get off track and lose sight of our purpose. There will be days when you need to remind yourself of these simple words, 'This is my purpose, this is what I'm paid to do'.

Are you familiar with the term grounded as it relates to electricity? In electrical engineering it is used to reference a common return path for electric currents back to a direct physical connection to the Earth (wikipedia).

Your home probably has grounded outlets to protect from power surges that can result in damage to you or your belongings.

Similarly, a mission statement can act as a ground wire when work seems out of control. It brings you back to earth so to speak and is a reminder of *why* we do *what* we do. Being grounded provides a sense of stability.

Like vision, there are many different definitions and opportunities for overcomplicating this step. And, like vision, articulating and communicating the overall mission of the organization is the responsibility for top leaders. All too often the mission is poorly articulated and doesn't get filtered throughout the organization.

Like many of the components that comprise the strategic level, the mission is at risk for becoming overcomplicated, watered down, and meaningless. The mission becomes another box to check off on the strategic plan.

In the 2010 TED Talk, How Leaders Inspire Action, Simon Sinek provided clarity around this elusive topic with the simple sentence "People don't buy what you do, they buy why you do it".

Sinek goes on to illustrate by sharing Apple's <u>why</u> which is 'we challenge the status quo'. Sinek explains the <u>why</u> as your cause, belief, or purpose. I call this the mission.

The difference between vision and mission is that mission often, but not always, involves emotion and vision is usually a concrete idea. You often hear the words passion, desire, calling, driving force, or purpose when discussing the topic of mission. Whereas, vision is usually equated to a place or a destination.

While not specifically mentioned as their mission statement, the story behind Zappos is a good example. From the Zappos.com website (http://www.zappos.com/d/about-zappos):

> The original idea was to create a web site that offered the absolute best

selection in <u>shoes</u> in terms of <u>brands</u>, styles, colors, sizes, and widths. (Primary purpose = offer the best selection of shoes)

It goes on to say that the reason the idea sparked was because the founder wanted <u>a better way of buying shoes online</u> (Mission = why). Zappos started with the desire for convenience.

That is a mission you can get your head around. If the overall mission of the company is to create a better way to buy shoes online, every department and every individual involved in the delivery of the service should be able to make the connection about how the work they do supports the mission.

Zappos is known for their customer service and ease of doing business. If you are customer service rep your mission might be to deliver the best customer experience possible and that would connect to the overall mission of creating a better way to buy shoes online.

Think of the small business owner who sacrifices time, money, and stability to build a business that may or may not take off. What energizes a business owner to make the sacrifices to start a business?

It isn't just about profitability, although every business owner dreams of making it big some day.

Why did the company begin in the first place? Was it just to make money or was there a bigger purpose behind it? What makes them get up every day in the face of adversity and uncertainty?

There has to be a passion or meaning behind what they are doing in order to make it through the certain ups and downs that comes with starting a business.

Many small business owners work a regular job while waiting for their new venture to take off or rely on the stability of revenue from one business to fund a second business.

If you calculate the number of hours put in vs. the take home pay it becomes clear that there has to be an internal drive that pushes them.

The partners of Aggressive Hydraulics know this all too well. President Paul Johnson's mission was born out of a desire to create job security. But, in order to get to that point they had to grow through a period of uncertainty as they were building the business. Any endeavor takes time to take hold and Aggressive Hydraulics was no different. Controller Wes Maack said if it was going to work there was no going half way, it was all or nothing. The partners took a significant risk by putting up everything they had and were willing to go months without taking a paycheck because they believed so much in their mission and their ability to make it a reality. They sacrificed personal and financial security in the short term for a long term reward and it paid off. What are you willing to give up in the short term to achieve what you want in the long term?

Writing The Mission Statement

To put in writing what you stand for isn't an easy task. You may feel a sense of hesitation. You may have to resist a strong urge to play it safe and go with a vague, long-winded statement that doesn't really mean anything. Remember, simple is best.

If you work for an organization with a long history, begin by finding the reason the original founder started it in the first place. It might be more difficult to determine the original reasons why the company was started but it could be interesting to dig in to the history.

I have been the founding member of several different organizations and every time a group started up the mission was born out of a desire to fill a need that was missing. One group I was part of forming was a networking group and our mission was to 'connect, educate, and inform women business professionals'. There was no other networking group providing this service in our area and we wanted to fill the void.

I was also a founding member of my small town's local chamber of commerce. The mission of the East Bethel Chamber of Commerce is to 'facilitate business relationships and opportunities'.

Notice the words used in both of the statements above – connect, educate, inform, facilitate, relationships – they are emotional words.

Microsoft's mission is a good example: At **Microsoft**, our **mission** is to enable people and businesses throughout the world to realize their full potential.

Enable, realize, full potential – there's passion in those words.

The components of a mission statement are:

1. verb

2. who or what

3. about

Use active verbs, specify who or what will be affected, and about what you are pursuing.

Verb	Who or What	About
Educate	Consumers	Importance of auto

		insurance
Enable, realize	People and Businesses	Their full potential
Make a better way	Consumers	Buy shoes online
Challenge	Status quo	
Push	Myself	Improve every day

Use the exercise as a way to get the ideas down on paper and don't worry about structure at this point or if the words don't fit perfectly. You can craft it into a succinct sentence later.

Apple's mission is to challenge the status quo. Notice there's is missing the 'who or what' component. They are still doing okay.

Let's put this to the test. Earlier we determined that Zappos *vision* is to create a website with the best selection of shoes online. Then we said their *mission* is to make a better way of buying shoes online.

If we worked at Zappos we might ask ourselves the following two questions to see if we're connecting our work to the vision and mission:

1. Is the work I'm doing helping to create a better way of buying shoes online?

2. Is the work I'm doing supporting the vision of creating a website with the best selection of shoes online?

In other words, do I know why (making a better way) I'm doing what (buying shoes online) I'm doing? The answer is yes.

If the leader sets the vision, who should set the mission for the organization, division, department, team, and individual? The people who are responsible for completing the work. It's human nature for people to put more energy into their own ideas. This is a perfect place to make the connection.

Use the following guide to generate ideas for your mission. Write down as many different words as you can think of in each column. Don't worry about crafting the perfect sentence as this point. Just brainstorm as many different words as you can. After you've exhausted your vocabulary, select the best ones from each column and make a sentence out of it.

Verb	Who	What
Provide	My team	Opportunities for growth and development

The example below is a solid univeral mission statement that could apply to all leaders in all organizations:

Provide opportunities for the growth and development of my team.

That little statement is something you can ground yourself in and use as a daily checkpoint to ensure you are doing your job. It really is that simple.

Make the Connection - Communicate and Cascade

Make the connection by communicating and cascading the mission throughout the organization from top to bottom. Starting at the top, share the mission during all employee meetings and in meetings with direct reports. Use the mission as a baseline for showing progress and supporting decisions.

Whenever possible, the leaders should talk about the mission and its history to their employees. Aggressive Hydraulics mission of creating a secure environment for everyone is stirring and inspiring and directly affects the employees. Keeping the mission front of mind reminds everyone of *why* they are doing *what* they are doing.

Mid-level managers can take the same steps as outlined above to communicate and cascade the mission to their departments. Keep the mission in the forefront of discussions during staff meetings. When announcing change, make the connection to show how the change supports the overall mission. Look for ways to connect the mission to the work the team is doing.

Cascade the mission by creating a mission for your own area of responsibility. If the overall mission is to educate consumers about the importance of auto insurance, the mission for the customer service department might be to provide thorough and accurate information to their customers. That department mission has a direct connection to the overall mission of education consumers.

What if you are a director or manager at a company that does not have an overall mission in place? View it for what it is, an opportunity to create a sense of purpose for your team. There is no harm in developing a department specific mission for your team.

Leaders at every level should take on this responsibility for their own area regardless if it is being done at the level above. Ideally, there is a mission for the organization as a whole but even if there is a poorly articulated mission or none at all, you can still create one for your area.

Good, Better, or Best?

It's been said that the good is the enemy of the best. That means it can be easy to settle for good enough rather than taking the time and energy into being the best.

'How much better could we be?'

GOOD

Verbally share the mission at company-wide employee meetings and publish the overall organizational mission on the company website, in marketing material, corporate reports, and in the lobby.

BETTER

Share at meetings and develop and display department specific mission statements in the department area.

While the overall vision for the organization is established by the leaders, it is critical that department specific missions are dictated by the people doing the work. People put more energy into their own ideas and getting the team involved ensures buy-in.

I distinctly remember the look of pride on the faces of my team when they hung their completed mission statement on the wall of their work area. I provided the initial direction, and corporate credit card so they could hash it out over lunch, and they had full authority to make it their own, and they did.

BEST

Talk about it, develop department specific mission statements, and visually display the cascading mission for each area of the organization from top to bottom for internal use.

 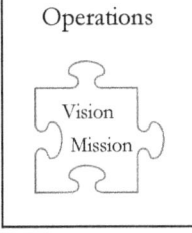 

Key Concepts

- Mission statements keep you grounded.
- Write the mission statement in one sentence and include a verb, who or what, and about.
- The people responsible for carrying out the mission should write it to ensure buy-in.
- Cascade the mission and share it internally.

Don't wait to be great. Create one for your team and yourself regardless of whether it has been done at the level above you.

Notes

Notes

_____
_____
_____
_____
_____
_____
_____
_____
_____
_____
_____
_____
_____
_____
_____
_____
_____
_____
_____
_____
_____
_____
_____
_____
_____
_____
_____

CHAPTER 4

BELIEF SYSTEMS AS BOUNDARIES

Your actions speak so loudly, I cannot hear what you say.

– Ralph Waldo Emerson

While vision is our primary purpose and mission is a reminder of why, core values are the belief systems that create boundaries. They are the guides that bridge the gap between vision and mission. Core value help everyone stay on course.

In the book *Traction,* core values are defined as 'a small set of vital and timeless guiding principles for your company'.

When everyone is demonstrating the core values, there is no need to advertise what they are. It should be evident by the team's actions. In fact, you shouldn't even have to tell people what your values are, they should know just by watching how you operate. If the core values are not lived, you as the leader have to decide what the consequences will be.

An employee who worked at a company that had The Golden Rule as a core value learned the hard way that they were serious about living the core values. In a moment of frustration, the employee sent out a derogatory email about a customer to the entire company and was promptly fired.

A wealth management firmed based out of New York has four guiding principles that support their primary purpose of being *the new standard in wealth management*. The four guiding principles are: Independent Advice; Direct Relationships; Planning and Investment Expertise; and Partnership Values.

They demonstrate the core value of Direct Relationships by assigning not one, but two, partners to every client account to ensure attention to their needs.

Unfortunately, many organizations have a list of core values that don't really mean anything. Almost every organization has their core values printed and hanging on a wall in a frame somewhere, with the vision and mission statement, or even painted on the walls to show real commitment. But do they mean anything? Too often they don't.

Every leader knows that an organization needs core values because every leadership book says so. Creating a set of core values that have no meaning and are just there to fill some kind of conventional requirement are a waste of time.

The owner of a once successful company who found himself near the brink of becoming obsolete was revamping his overall strategy in an effort to become relevant again. Part of the strategy included a new vision statement and set of core values.

A nice vision statement was crafted that stated they were the trusted resource in their industry. His philosophy was that if you told people long enough and loud enough that you were the trusted resource they would believe you, regardless of your actions.

He insisted on including trust and integrity in the five core values. Unfortunately, his actions did not match his words. One day he stood in the office ranting at his wife, who worked there part-time, while another employee was on the phone making sales calls less than 20 feet away. Trust and integrity? Not so much.

You can say whatever you want to the outside world but if you aren't living it on the inside you'll never get there.

What are your core values? What matters to you

and your team? What do you actually stand for? Not what you think other people would be impressed by but what do your daily actions actually convey to others inside and outside your organization? Be original here. Don't just put something down because you think it sounds good.

Core values are another piece of the puzzle that connect the team to the vision. They are actions taken on a daily basis that guide the mission and advances the organization toward the vision. Core values bridge the gap between mission and vision.

For example, if your mission is to <u>inspire others to realize their potential</u> and your vision is to <u>be the #1 service provider in your industry</u>, you would choose core values that keep you on track.

You may select quality as a core value because providing quality services that make a difference in the lives of the consumer will move you toward becoming #1.

Make the Connection:

Vision	Mission	Core Value
Be #1 provider	Inspire others to realize their potential	Quality

Win Olympic gold medal	Improve every day	Practice
Create cutting-edge technology	Challenge the status quo	Innovation

Defining Your Core Values

Who should write the core values? The leadership team should define the core values for the overall organization.

Managers along with their team can come up with core values for their department that tie into the overall values. Like mission, core values are a component that requires buy-in from the people who have to demonstrate the values through their actions so it is critical to involve them in the discussion. In the case of writing core values, the key people are the people who you expect to act on them. Involve everyone.

Tony Hsieh, CEO of Zappos.com, a company that consistently emerges as a great example of how to keep this thing simple, emailed his entire organization to gather individual feedback on what matters. By soliciting input over the course of a year he identified 10 core values that all employees are expected to live up to.

The Zappos way of doing things has become so successful that it has become an institution in and of itself for teaching other leaders who to do it.

You can quickly get a list of ideas for core values by having a brainstorming session in a regular staff meeting. You don't have to complete the entire exercise in one sitting. In fact, sometimes it's better to do it in phases to give people time to absorb the ideas, let the ideas soak in, then come back to refine them. Here are three simple steps for developing your team's core values (CV):

1. Gather ideas - Start by asking the team to contribute one word to describe what matters in their day to day work. Examples might include responsiveness, teamwork, or accuracy. Write the responses down on a whiteboard or flip chart so they are visible to everyone. If the group is reserved and is reluctant to verbalize their reponses, have them write their ideas on a post-it note, one idea per note and gather the information that way.

2. Vote on ideas - Once you have a good list have each person vote for their top three reponses and take the top five overall picks.

3. Identify demonstrable actions for each CV – After the team has identified the top three to five values, it's time to discuss actions that everyone will commit to.

This is where you might take a break, give everyone time to let the ideas soak in, and come back later to finish.

Because core values are something to be practiced in real-time, use words that you can put into action. Avoid a laundry list of rules that explain what it means to act on each core value. Be cautious about using the old standby's trust and integrity unless you can give specific examples of how to put them into action. How do you demonstrate trust? How do you demonstrate integrity? Most people would say 'do the right thing'. That's too subjective. What is the right thing? There is another saying, never trust anyone who has to tell you that they are honest. In other words, be wary of anyone who tells you the check is in the mail.

Core values that can be demonstrated readily by everyone are the most useful. Friendly is one example of a core value that might be appropriate for a service based business. It isn't too hard to come up with a few specific attributes for friendliness: Look people in the eye, smile, and acknowledge others with a greeting are a few easy ways to demonstrate friendliness.

How about innovation? In what ways could you demonstrate innovation? Number of new products rolled out each year, investing in research, and using the most up to date equipment and technology, might be a few ways to put innovation into action.

Learning might be a core value. Is there room in the budget for training, does everyone have the opportunity to learn if they want to, do you have a cross-training program, a leadership development program, a defined career path with resources to assist those who want to move up? How could you demonstrate learning as a core value?

Core Value	Specific Action or Behavior
Service	Respond to inquiries within specified time frames
Innovation	Introduce 20 new products annually
Learning	Attend one training each quarter

Avoid getting too detailed here. One concrete idea is all that is needed. If you can't commit to the idea, then get rid of it. For instance, if having every employee attend one class every quarter to demonstrate learning as a core value isn't feasible then do something else.

Set your team up for success. As the leader, provide adequate resources to support the core values. For example, if innovation is an overall organizational value, is the budget appropriate for research & development and any capital expenditures?

If you are the department manager and learning is one of your team's values, do you have a sufficient line item for education in your budget? Get creative if your resources are limited.

I worked at one organization where learning was a high priority and I always had a healthy budget for training and development. When I moved to another organization that did not have learning as a high priority, because they were focused on other things, my budget was limited. I got creative and did more training in-house. Instead of sending team members to external workshops and seminars, I purchased books for everyone and facilitated lunch 'n learns. Understand your limitations and communicate those to your team so they know the constraints you're under. Otherwise they could assume you're withholding opportunities.

Communicate Like a Boss, discusses how to set job standards for performance and behavior. Instead of reinventing the wheel, why not use the core values to demonstrate the behavioral standards you are looking for. After all, the connected company is consistent from top to bottom. The annual performance evaluation is a good place to look for the values you want people to demonstrate. You may notice a correlation between the core values and the performance review. Most performance evaluation forms include a section on core competencies. Keep it simple. Make the connection. The reason people hate performance reviews is because no one talks about them throughout the year. It's becoming more popular to do away with the annual performance review and opt for ongoing conversations throughout the year. That's a terrible idea. If a manager can't talk to their team at least once a year about their performance what are the chances that they will talk to them more frequently? A manager's failure to communicate is no reason to eliminate the annual performance appraisal altogether. Elimating performance evaluations is treating the symptom instead of the problem.

Core values are one of the easiest aspects of alignment to measure, if you have identified practical ways to demonstrate them.

Make the Connection – Communicate and Cascade

It's not hard to make decisions once you know what your values are.

– Roy Disney

Make the connection by communicating and cascading the core values throughout the organization from top to bottom. Starting at the top, share core values during employee meetings. Use the core values as a baseline for identifying desired behaviors. Keep core values front and center to ensure alignment. Cascade core values by having the next level create a set of core values for their area.

Mid-level managers can take the same steps as outlined above to communicate and cascade core values to their departments. Keep the core values in the forefront of discussions during staff meetings and when giving performance feedback. Look for ways to connect the core values to the work the team is doing.

What if you are a director or manager at a company that does not have overall core values in place? View it for what it is, an opportunity to create them for your team. There is no harm in defining core values for your team. Leaders at every level should take on this responsibility for their own area regardless if it is being done at the level above.

Good, Better, or Best?

It's been said that the good is the enemy of the best. That means it can be easy to settle for good enough rather than taking the time and energy into being the best.

'How much better could we be?'

GOOD

Share the core values at an employee meeting and publish the overall organizational core values on the company website, in marketing material, corporate reports, and in the lobby.

BETTER

Talk about them, develop and display department specific core values statements in the department area and incorporate them into performance discussions.

BEST

Talk about them, develop them, and visually display the cascading core values for each area of the organization from top to bottom for internal use and periodically check in with the team to find out how they are demonstrating the core values.

Slot a few minutes on the department meeting agenda for each person to share one way in which they have demonstrated a core value in the last quarter. For example, if you used learning as a core value and the action was to attend a training session every quarter, have everyone share the training they completed.

Go above and beyond by having each person write down how they demonstrated a core value over the last quarter on a large note card and post the responses on the wall with the vision and mission.

Key Concepts

- Core values are basic guiding principles
- Actions speak louder than words
- Each core value should correspond to demonstratable behaviors
- Use quarterly check-ins with the team to discuss how each person is demonstrating at least one core value and display the responses in a visible area

Don't wait to be great. Come up with a list of 3 – 5 core values at your level regardless of what others are doing.

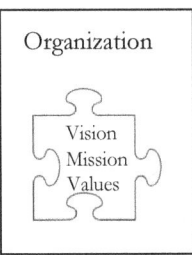

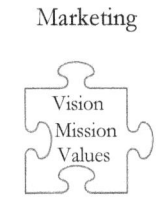 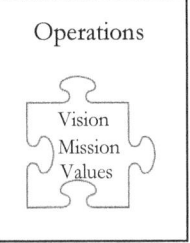 

Key Concepts

- Core values are basic guiding principles
- Actions speak louder than words
- Each core value should correspond to demonstratable behaviors
- Use quarterly check-ins with the team to discuss how each person is demonstrating at least one core value and display the responses in a visible area

Don't wait to be great. Come up with a list of 3 – 5 core values at your level regardless of what others are doing.

Notes

Notes

_____

_____

_____

_____

_____

_____

_____

_____

_____

_____

_____

_____

_____

_____

_____

_____

_____

_____

_____

_____

_____

_____

_____

_____

_____

_____

_____

_____

CHAPTER 5

GUIDE THE GROUP CULTURE

Culture eats strategy for breakfast.

– Peter Drucker

Vision tells us what our primary purpose is, mission tells us why we do what we do, core values tell us what we believe in, and culture is who we are.

Culture is the collective personality of the organization. Teams are made up of a wide variety of individual personalities and when those personalities come together in the melting pot of the workplace the culture of the company is formed.

Culture is an important component at the strategic level because it has wide-ranging implications that affect dealings both internally and externally.

The definition of corporate culture, according to

Investopedia.com, is:

> The beliefs and behaviors that determine how a company's employees and management interact and handle outside business transactions. Often, corporate culture is implied, not expressly defined, and develops organically over time from the cumulative traits of the people the company hires. A company's culture will be reflected in its dress code, business hours, office setup, employee benefits, turnover, hiring decisions, treatment of clients, client satisfaction and every other aspect of operations.

Culture is different from vision, mission, and values in that it isn't something that the leader consciously writes out, shares with everyone and says this is who we are now go out and act like it.

Culture does not develop overnight, it evolves over time. Because the forming and shaping of culture is a slow process a leader may be surprised to turn around one day and realize they are not who they thought they were. A leader must possess a degree of awareness of self and others to notice the almost invisible shifts that impact the whole in either a good or bad way. The old adage is true, one bad apple can spoil the bunch.

Monique Winston, CEO of Optima Lender

Services, summed it up so well with this statement 'If you do not develop your corporate culture it will develop itself. Corporate culture doesn't happen by accident and if it does, you're taking a risk'.

One of the reasons core values are a critical component of alignment is that they provide boundaries for behaviors that shape the organizational culture. However, having the core values in writing doesn't guarantee adherence.

Core values are subject to interpretation or being ignored so the leader must remain alert and aware to what's developing. If they don't, factions can crop up that do not align with the overall culture and over time you end up with a culture you did not want.

An organization is like a neighborhood comprised of many individual homes. Imagine a neighborhood on a tree lined cul-de-sac with eight homes. While the home styles are similar, and everyone has two cars in the garage and maybe a pool in the back, if you looked inside each of those houses they would each have a unique dynamic.

You might find a home that is the social hub of the neighborhood, a conservative home, a liberal home, a dysfunctional drama-filled home, an adventurous home, a domineering home, and a busybody home, just to name a few. Inside each of these homes is another set of personalities made up of the people who live there.

While each of the homes within the neighborhood are different, the neighborhood as a whole has a personality that could be described as modern, upper-middle-class, family-oriented, with room to grow.

That's how it is in organizations. The neighborhood itself is the organization, the homes are the departments within the organization, and the people who live in the homes are the individuals who make up the teams. If one of those homes in the neighborhood begins to dominate, you might find yourself in a neighborhood you don't want to be in.

At Aggressive Hydraulics, the partners are paying close attention to maintaining the culture they have purposefully and deliberately created for their organization. They learned first-hand how having a team spread out across separate facilities can breed different cultures. Before building a larger facility to accommodate their expanding business, they were located in three different buildings. Even though the physical distance wasn't great, each location had developed its own culture. When they brought everyone together under one roof there was a slight adjustment period as everyone settled in. It wasn't that the cultures were bad, but it did highlight the importance of aligning the team under one culture to create the security that is so important to the mission of the company. Looking into the future, they are conscious about maintaining one culture to keep the team connected.

Understanding and cultivating the right personality for your organization is important for two reasons:

1. Culture affects the ability to execute. You can have a well-defined vision, a perfectly articulated mission, and solid core values but if the personality as a whole is dysfunctional, it will be hard to execute on the strategy.

2. Culture affects the ability to get the best people on the team.

There are many signs of a dysfunctional team:

1. Refusal to change

2. Failure to take ownership

3. Hidden agendas, and unhealthy alliances

In the workplace, change isn't optional, it's mandatory in order to maintain a competitive advantage. Sure, some organizations limp along doing the same old thing year after year. They get by and think they are doing okay but they don't really grow. A question every business leader needs to ask themselves, regardless of how much success they've already achieved is, how much better could we be?

You would not be reading this if you weren't interested in improving.

Failure to take ownership is another sign of a dysfunctional culture. A team who is afraid to take responsibility is not going to execute. Execution requires commitment to the plan. Are people truly free to challenge the status quo without fear of retaliation? I once witnessed a CEO unleash his rage on a vice president in a senior management meeting and it sent a clear message to keep your thoughts to yourself.

Hidden agendas and political alliances go hand in hand. It is impossible to move forward when you have secret alliances of two or three people trying to steer the direction away from the primary purpose. If you think this might be a problem in your organization pay attention to who is trying to steer the discussion away from the agenda at your next meeting.

The most telling sign of alliances are the people who squirrel away to someone's office for the 'meeting after the meeting' they just tried to derail. These behind closed doors recaps with two or three of the key players are keeping you from executing on the strategy. If you confront them on it they will say they are collaborating. Don't buy it. They have their own plan.

The leader's influence is great when it comes to culture because it is shaped by what is allowed and what is not. Top down leadership forms the personality. A leader who ignores bad behavior is providing fertile ground for the seeds of an unhealthy culture to bloom.

Understanding the culture of the organization is also important when it comes to job fit. Have you ever been in a workplace where you felt you didn't fit it in? Not because of the skill required but because of the work environment?

Someone who is independent and prefers autonomy is not going to thrive in a parental culture where check ins are required before decisions can be made.

Someone who is very relational and values having fun at work will not fit well in a heads-down, task-focused culture.

There is no right or wrong when it comes to organizational culture, but it is important to know what yours is so you can hire people who can do their best work.

Examples of culture clashes:

- A person who is bottom line focused may not enjoy sitting through skits at all-staff meetings. They want to get down to business and get back to work.

- Someone who is relationship focused will be miserable in an environment that does not promote team work and collaboration.

- A structured person will not thrive in an environment where it's normal to do everything at the last minute without a detailed plan.

- Someone who values stability will not fare well in a chaotic environment with frequent change.

This doesn't mean that different styles can never mix. In fact, you need a mix of all types to make an organization run especially when it breaks down into departments.

The marketing department will likely have a different overall personality than the finance department. Even the most hard-driving, results oriented person enjoys a celebration from time to time. Find the right mix and balance it out.

The key is to know your culture and hire people who fit. If you don't, they won't be happy and neither will you. In order to do that you must first identify the personality of your organization which we'll do next.

How to identify the organizational culture

What would happen if you called a meeting and asked your team to describe the organizational culture? Not much. You would get a lot of blank stares or maybe some vague feel good responses about providing exceptional service.

It's not an easy question to answer but there is a simple and effective way to get a consensus of the personality of your organization by asking the following question…

> *If our organization (division, department, or team) were a car, what kind of car would it be and why?*

It may seem a little silly but it is revealing. As an added bonus it's a good team building exercise. Ask them to describe the car down to the smallest detail. What color is it? Does it have cloth or leather interior? Is it new or used? Does it come fully loaded or with factory accessories? Is it powered by diesel fuel, regular fuel, or is it an electric vehicle? They must explain the reason behind the details. The rationale reveals the culture.

Whatever they come up with, don't take it personally. It's just information. If the team describes the organization as an old junker held together with duct tape that gives you a clear indication that there is an opportunity for making some improvements.

You might wonder what this has to do with culture. Everything. Business philosopher Jim Rohn said we become like the five people we spend the most time with so we better be sure we are hanging with the right crowd. People who live or work in stagnant, hopeless, downtrodden circumstances become stagnant, hopeless and downtrodden.

People who live or work in a fast-paced, optimistic, forward moving environment are more likely to share their ideas and take chances which is necessary for growth.

This exercise works because a car is something that nearly everyone can relate to. They don't have to be familiar with specific makes and models to describe the features. If your team has any concerns about being honest with this exercise, let them work on it privately and turn in their results anonymously. You can't fix what you aren't aware of so be open to hearing what they have to say. If you are not pleased with the results, don't hold it against the messenger, take it for what it is, an opportunity to improve.

Here are some actual examples of what this looks like in action:

The leadership team of a non-profit was experiencing conflict with the board of directors regarding the direction (vision) of the organization. The board wanted them to be more contemporary and cutting edge, while the leadership team desired a more traditional, down to earth culture. The leadership team was having a hard time putting their ideas into words and this exercise helped them paint a clear picture of what they were all about. While the board may have viewed the organization as a Tesla, the leadership team and staff, saw themselves as an extended cab tan Chevy Silverado with cloth interior, heavy duty towing capacity, and room for everyone. Quite a disconnect.

Another organization, a wealth management firm, described themselves as a fully loaded late model Buick. Navy blue with gold trim, and leather interior. They felt it conveyed a solid, conservative, but not cheap, image and the fact that it was a late model showed financial prudence. This exercise was conducted with six different groups of the leadership team and they all came to the same conclusion. That's a connected team.

A meeting with the human resources team at a private university uncovered a less positive viewpoint. Everyone agreed on the type of vehicle but the image wasn't great. I won't name the exact make and model, but the basic description was a luxury vehicle that looked great on the outside but needed a lot of work under the hood. The university was in the middle of a major leadership change and there was a strong current of anxiety and uncertainty permeating the culture. Everyone wondered if it was all going to break down and leave them stranded on the side of the road. Lots of disconnect going on there.

So what do you do if you think your organization is a Mercedes Benz and everyone else thinks it's a Ford Pinto? It all starts at the top. Start by identifying the actions you have taken, or not taken, that have created the environment. If you find that your organization has developed into a 'not my fault' culture you need to change that into a culture of accountability.

Examine the leadership at the top of each area you are responsible for. Do you have people in leadership positions who are instilling the wrong culture? The most common ways this happens are: not holding people accountable; not enforcing policy; flip flopping on decisions; and not supporting the decisions of the management team below them.

Personal cell phone use during work hours is a big problem for many organizations these days. One group of supervisors at a manufacturing facility were wracking their brains trying to figure out how to get their workers to stop using their cell phones on the production floor. Not only is it extremely dangerous, it violates company policy. They came up with all kinds of ideas for dealing with the issue except one-enforce the policy. The longer the policy was ignored the harder it became to deal with and the bigger the problem got. What developed was a culture of everyone doing what they want and constant push back. That kind of environment is hard to manage and does not attract good workers.

The reason many leaders don't like to enforce policy is that they don't want to be the bad guy. Smart leaders know it isn't about being a good guy or a bad guy. It's about knowing what type of leadership style is appropriate to a given situation. Policy enforcement requires a directive leadership style. Policies that aren't enforced should be eliminated all together. Either have a policy or don't have one but if you are going to have it, enforce it. Of course, you don't want to regulate every move that's made so choose carefully.

If you notice leaders in your organization who are doing things that create a difficult culture, you need to fix it fast. The leader always has ultimate responsibility for everything that is happening under their charge. The higher you are on the leadership chain, the more responsibility you have.

Like changing the course of a ship, changing the personality of an organization requires small degrees of change over a long period of time. A ship, unlike a small speedboat cannot make sharp turns, it would break in half. Remember, the culture didn't happen overnight, it evolved over time. To change something very large requires a series of incremental steps.

Because people are who they are, it's unlikely they are going to change. This is why you will often see massive overhauls of personnel when new leaders take over. The new leader typically brings in their team because they already work together in sync.

Remember the widow who took over the truck dealership? She learned that when putting structure in place, doing too much too fast can create challenges. It takes time to introduce change, and one of the big blessings for her is a stable workforce that has been around a long time. That also means a lot of set ideas about how things should be done. The lesson learned is that it takes time to get new language and ideas instilled. Where it would be common for many leaders to either force the change or give up entirely, she reviewed what needed to be done differently and made the necessary adjustments to keep moving the strategy forward. Now she does more guiding than directing which is increasing accountability and buy-in.

Make the Connection – Communicate and Cascade

---

*There's no magic formula for great company culture.
The key is just to treat your staff how you would like
to be treated.*

– Richard Branson

Make the connection by communicating and cascading the desired traits of the culture throughout the organization from top to bottom. Starting at the top, share the traits of the culture during all employee meetings and in meetings with direct reports.

Cascade the culture by having the next level identify the culture of their area. Most importantly, lead by example. Demonstrate the traits you want everyone to live up to.

Mid-level managers can take the same steps as outlined above to communicate and cascade the culture to their departments. Management can identify the culture of their area by doing the exercise of asking 'If our department were a car, what kind of car would we be?' in a department meeting.

Good, Better, or Best?

It's been said that the good is the enemy of the best. That means it can be easy to settle for good enough rather than taking the time and energy into being the best.

'How much better could we be?'

GOOD

Identify the overall culture of the organization.

BETTER

Identify the overall culture and the culture at each department level.

BEST

Identify the overall culture, the department culture, and visually display the culture at each level of the organization from top to bottom for internal use.

Create a visual by displaying a picture of the kind of car each area came up with in a common area along with vision, mission, and core values.

One exception, if any team comes up with a junker held together with duct tape, fix the problems before displaying the picture.

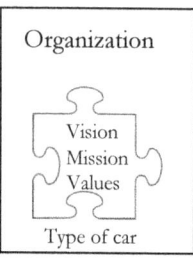

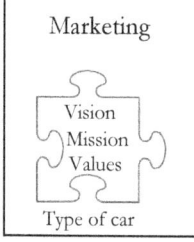 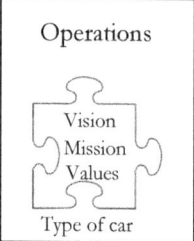 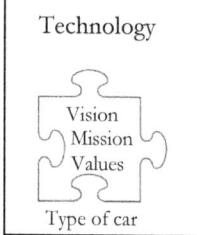

Key Concepts

- Culture is the collective personality of all the people in the organization
- The leader is responsible for influencing the culture
- There is no right or wrong culture as long as results are achieved
- Check for alignment at each level with the exercise, If our company (or division, department, or team) were a car, what kind of car would it be and why?

Don't wait to be great. Do this with your team regardless of what is being done in other areas of the organization.

Notes

_____
_____
_____
_____
_____
_____
_____
_____
_____
_____
_____
_____
_____
_____
_____
_____
_____
_____
_____
_____
_____
_____
_____
_____
_____
_____
_____

Notes

CHAPTER 6

ACHIEVE THE PRIMARY PURPOSE

Setting goals is the first step in turning the invisible into the visible.

– Tony Robbins

Establishing one year organizational goals is the fifth way smart leaders build strong organizations. If vision is the primary purpose, mission is why we do it, core values are what we believe, culture is who we are, then goals are how we fulfill our primary purpose.

When you are talking about overall business strategy the goals can start at twenty years, then ten years, then five, and finally one year goals.

For the purpose of this book we'll focus on the one year goals. Goals set at the strategic level are typically going to be related to things like revenue, market share, and profitability because that is exactly what the top level of leadership is responsible for.

According to *Strategic Speed: Mobilize People, Accelerate Execution*, only 30% of strategic initiatives fully succeed, on time. That doesn't seem like a great return on investment for all the time and effort required to create the strategic plan. Many factors play into the failure to execute but the one that cannot be overlooked is overcomplication of the plan and the failure to make a good connection.

At the intersection of strategy and execution you will find the one year goals. The one year goals are crucial to the success of the overall strategy and this is where most disconnects takes place.

One year goals make the long-term vision manageable. Communicating the long-term vision without incremental steps would be overwhelming.

Imagine an individual contributor being given Microsoft's early vision of putting a computer on every desk and in every home, and being told to go make it happen. Your head would spin. Where would you start?

Think of the one year goals as the baton in a relay race. A relay team is typically made up of four individuals, each doing their part before handing the baton to the next person. Like a relay team, one year goals are handed from leader to senior leader to manager to individual contributor for execution on the strategy.

Unfortunately, in many organizations someone is left hanging out on the track waiting for the leader to come around the turn and make the hand off. The leader never comes and they lose the race. Or, there isn't a clean handoff and the baton drops causing the team to fall behind and lose their competitive advantage.

How to Establish One Year Goals

You may be familiar with the SMART goal setting method. Try the MAT method instead. MAT is smarter than SMART goals because it streamlines the goal into the essential requirements of a metric, an action, and a timeframe. Anytime you can streamline a process you automatically become smarter. SMART stands for specific, measurable, achievable, relevant, and time-based. If your goal meets the three criteria of the **MAT** process it will naturally be specific, achievable, and relevant.

Metric – what is the measure? Every goal needs to have a number or a percent attached to it. If you can't measure it, it isn't a goal.

Always start by determining the current metric. Too many people go about setting unnecessary goals because they don't know what the current result is.

Why spend time trying to improve something that's already working? There is some truth to the old saying 'if it ain't broke don't fix it'. Focus on improving things that really need it first. Don't set a goal if there is nothing to improve.

Action – what specific action is being taken. Use verbs. *Earn* 'x' amount of revenue.

Time – when it will be complete. This would naturally be the end of the year for the one year goal. If you realize that the goal is too big to complete in that time frame, refine the goal until it is manageable.

The MAT process drills goals down to their finest point leaving no room for ambiguity. Each section is either complete or it isn't. Following this very simple process will help you determine the best goals. Goals should be crisp, clear, and concise. Aim for stating the goal in one sentence.

Metric	Action	Timeframe
$25,000,000	Earn	12/31
65 new locations	Open	12/31
20 new hires	Add	12/31

Written out, these goals would read as:

- Earn $25,000,000 in revenue by December 31, 20__
- Open 65 new locations by December 31, 20__
- Add 20 new hires by December 31, 20__

Warning: It will be very tempting to overcomplicate the process. Resist the urge to get into details about how these goals will be accomplished. At this level you don't need to worry about *how* it will get done, your job is only to decide *what* will be done.

You might look at those short sentences think 'that can't be it, there must be more, it's not enough!'. You will be tempted to add unnecessary words to make them seem stronger. Stop. They are just fine the way they are and are ready to move to the next stage for implementation.

Make the Connection – Communicate and Cascade

The one year goals are the most critical component of executing the plan. Even if none of the other priniciples are communicated and cascaded, goals must be.

Cascading the goals through all levels of the organization is how strategy gets executed. At each level the goals become more granular to the point where the goals being worked on at the base level are generating the right activities to ensure the goals at the highest level are achieved.

Make the connection by communicating and cascading the one year goals throughout the organization from top to bottom. As soon as the executive leadership team has the one year organizational goals in place, they should pass these off to the next level and ask 'What ideas do you have for supporting these goals within your respective areas of responsibility?'.

Next, mid-level managers will communicate and cascade the goals by establishing three to five goals for their area and pass the department goals to the team, asking individual team members 'What ideas do you have for supporting these goals?'. Each member of each team will write their own goals to support the overall organization goals.

What if you work for a company that does not have goals in place coming down from the top? View it for what it is, an opportunity for your team. There is no harm in defining goals for your team. Leaders at every level should take on goal setting for their own area regardless if it is being done at the level above.

Good, Better, or Best?

It's been said that the good is the enemy of the best. That means it can be easy to settle for good enough rather than taking the time and energy into being the best.

'How much better could we be?'

GOOD

Establish one year organizational goals and verbally share them at an all staff meeting and in company-wide communication.

BETTER

Establish one year organizational goals *and* develop department specific goals that support the goals of the level above.

BEST

Establish one year organizational goals, *and* develop one year department goals, *and* visually display the cascading goals for each area of the organization from top to bottom for internal use.

Increase transparency and improve the odds for success by posting every single goal from the top organizational goal down to individual goals in a shared common space along with vision, mission, core values, and culture to show how each goal supports the next level goal.

That is how you create a connected team from top to bottom and bridge the gap between strategy and execution. Please note the operative word at each handoff is 'ask'. People will always put more energy and effort into their own ideas so take care to avoid the common pitfall of dictating what the next level goals should be.

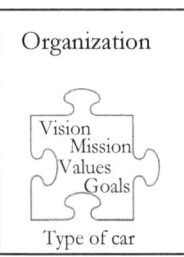

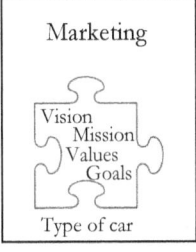 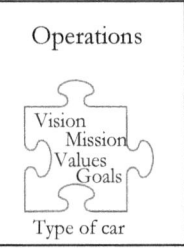 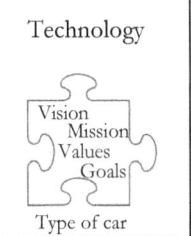

Key Concepts

- One year goals are the critical handoff between strategy and execution
- Use the MAT process = metric, action, timeframe
- Aim for 3 – 5 goals
- Cascase the goals through each level and have every single person in the organization create goals that support the organizational goal

Notes

Notes

_____

_____

_____

_____

_____

_____

_____

_____

_____

_____

_____

_____

_____

_____

_____

_____

_____

_____

_____

_____

_____

_____

_____

_____

_____

_____

_____

CHAPTER 7

STRATEGIC ALIGNMENT

Knowledge without action is just information.

The final piece to make the connection and build a strong organization is to hold everyone accountable to the process. A group that will not participate in the process is a sign of a weak connection. If not held accountable it will be like finishing a puzzle and realizing there is a missing piece. It will won't look quite right and it loses value.

Leaders at each level can use the following template to create the connection from top to bottom. Always keep in mind the philosophy that simple is better and remind people to not overcomplicate it.

Make the Connection – Strategic Alignment

Area of Responsibility

_____

Leader

_____

Date Completed _____

Date Shared With Next Level   _____

Vision

_____
_____
_____
_____

Mission

_____
_____
_____
_____

Core Values

	Core Value	Specific Actions
1.	_____	_____
2.	_____	_____
3.	_____	_____
4.	_____	_____
5.	_____	_____

Culture

If our area (group, department, team, etc.) were a car, what kind of a car would we be and why?

_____

_____

_____

_____

_____

_____

One Year Goals

1.	_____
2.	_____
3.	_____
4.	_____
5.	_____

Notes

_____
_____
_____
_____
_____
_____
_____
_____
_____
_____
_____
_____
_____
_____
_____
_____
_____
_____
_____
_____
_____
_____
_____
_____
_____
_____

Notes

Book Liz Uram to speak at your next event!

Contact Liz for your speaking and training needs. The topics covered in this book can be customized for your group and presented as a keynote, a breakout session, a multi-day event, or anything in between.

For availability and booking information, please visit www.lizuram.com or contact Liz directly at (612) 961-9801.

What others say:

> *The best class ever! I came in looking for one solution regarding one person and left with ways to work better with my team and others in my life. Truly life changing. Liz is very professional and has a great way of teaching.*
>
> *Liz's ability to quickly understand the core function of our department and identify specifics was impressive.*
>
> *All of the suggestions were real life situations that made it easy to relate to.*
>
> *She was able to deliver great actionable ideas and get the audience engaged, participating and laughing.*
>
> *She used many examples and connected with the audience very well. Her interaction with the group was outstanding. I highly recommend Ms. Uram in the future to anyone.*

Share Make the Connection with others!

This book makes a great gift for conference attendees, in-house training, and teams.

Purchase 50 or more copies and receive 50% off the retail price.

Email liz@lizuram.com or call (612) 961-9801 to order.

ABOUT THE AUTHOR

Liz Uram speaks to leaders, teams, and individuals on bridging the gap between strategy and execution and works one-on-one with people who need help putting their plans into action. She has over 15 years of experience practicing, studying, and teaching the leadership principles she shares with others. When she is not speaking, coaching, or conducting seminars, she enjoys spending time on the golf course, in her garden, and hanging out with family and friends.